ORPHIC SONGS

FIELD TRANSLATION SERIES 9

Dino Campana

ORPHIC SONGS

Translated by Charles Wright

Introduction by Jonathan Galassi

FIELD Translation Series 9

The following poems were published in magazines, and the author is grateful to their editors:

The Missouri Review: "La Verna," "Journey to Montevideo," "Autumn Garden," "In the Mountains," "Song of Darkness." *The Paris Review*: "The Night" *The Three Penny Review*: "Genoa Woman," "Toscanità," "Autumn Garden."

The author is also grateful to Carlo Pelliccia for his help, and especially grateful, again, to Vinio Rossi for his wise counsel.

The Montale essay is reprinted, with some changes, from *The Second Life of Art: Selected Essays of Eugenio Montale*, edited and translated by Jonathan Galassi, Ecco Press, 1982.

Publication of this book was made possible through a grant from the Ohio Arts Council.

Library of Congress Cataloging in Publication Data
  Campana, Dino (translated by Charles Wright)
  ORPHIC SONGS
  (The FIELD Translation Series; v. 9)
LC: 83-063448
ISBN: 09-32440-16-9
    09-32440-17-7 (paperback)

These translations are for J. G., whose cool hand has been on their feverish brow . . .

CONTENTS

A HYMN OF NON-ATTAINMENT
by Jonathan Galassi

Anyone who drives from Faenza to Florence
—through the rich, flat farms of Romagna up
into the wooded foothills of the Apennines
which form a natural barrier with Tuscany,
then across the stony yellow pastureland atop
the old mountains themselves and down on into
the valley of the Arno — will experience an es-
sential component of Dino Campana's poetry.
He was born in Marradi, a small town wedged
into the narrow valley of the Lamone River on
the Faenza side of the divide (though the town
belongs legally to the province of Florence). An
incessant wanderer all his adult life, he made
long walking trips in the historic and holy terri-
tory of the Casentino, the shell of mountains
stretching north and west of Arezzo where the
Arno begins. These places, along with the an-
cient cities of northern Italy — Florence, Bo-
logna, Faenza, Genoa —are evoked with great
sensual immediacy in the "musical, colored po-
etry" that constitutes one of the most radical
and pure moments in modern Italian literature.
In Campana's work, the primal elements of his
world —rock, wind, water, sky, sun, heat, night

and its lights, as well as women, song, and the greatest element of all, the immense Mediterranean in which everything else is formed and bathed — endlessly combine, dissolve, and reunite in the stream of patterns formed by his restless inspiration.

Campana is a unique case in Italian poetry, comparable in some ways to what Rimbaud is for the French or Hart Crane for our own tradition. As the critic Emilio Cecchi wrote, he "passed like a comet" across the firmament of Italian letters, leaving it astonished, though finally more or less unchanged, so idiosyncratic and eccentric was his contribution. Campana appeared in the midst of the great political, social, and cultural turmoil that the turn of the century was in Italy and throughout Europe, and in his own peculiar way he absorbed and expressed the multifarious influences of that moment, including symbolism, the Italian Twilight, and futurism, as well as Walt Whitman, Edgar Allan Poe, and Nietzsche. Out of all this, and from his own personal turbulence, he forged a powerful obsessive song, a violent pure poetry of undirected and thus unsatisfiable desire and need, which has a visionary, even hallucinatory intensity. The continuous, almost undifferentiated paean-lament that runs through the *Canti orfici* and much of the rest of his work, is certainly the harshest and most relentless lyric utterance in the history of a highly rationalized and convention-bound tradition. Eugenio Montale, the greatest twentieth-century continuator and interpreter of this tradition, whose own radicalism was much more internal and rationalized, liked to repeat the dictum of the baroque Jesuit poet Tommaso Ceva that poetry is "a dream dreamed in the presence of reason." But this balance, so strongly adhered to in Italian letters, is wildly off in Campana. For him the dream, the nightmare, is virtually everything.

Campana's poems are not really conventionally finished lyrics at all. At their most concise they are more like lyric fragments; more often, they are prose meditations or journal entries. They can be repetitive, obscure, contradictory, sometimes virtually inarticulate. Yet their very failure to communicate is tremendously effective in conveying the erotic and emotional blockage, the non-attainment, that is the true burden of Campana's work. Campana's failure to express is in a way the most expressive, the most universal thing about him. His poetry seems almost involuntary, and this may explain

11

why his work has left so few obvious traces. Writing of this urgency is impossible to imitate.

The futurists, too, had experimented, more willfully and manipulatively, with obscurity and the irrational, and Campana clearly learned from their work, but he took pains to dissociate himself from them. To him the futurists were "empty," and their poetry was lacking in genuineness. As he wrote to Bino Binazzi, who was preparing the second edition of the *Canti orfici* in 1928: "Every now and then I wrote bizarre poems but I was not a futurist. Futurist free verse is false, it is not harmonic. It is an improvisation without color or harmony. I was making a little art."

Campana's personal history is tragic. He was born in Marradi on August 20, 1885. His father was the principal of the local elementary school. His mother, who came from a well-to-do family, was, according to I. L. Salomon,[1] "an eccentric" who "used to wander up into the hills fingering her rosary, frequently forgetting to prepare dinner for her husband and children." Campana's emotional difficulties first became apparent in 1900, when, as his father later told one of his doctors, the adolescent demonstrated "a brutal, unhealthy impulsivity in the family, especially toward his mother."[2] It was at this point, too, that his wandering began. "I travelled a great deal," he wrote to Binazzi. "I was urged on by a kind of mania for wandering. A sort of instability forced me to change continually. . . . From the age of fifteen, a powerful nervousness took hold of me, and I couldn't live anywhere." In 1902, after studying intermittently in Turin and Carmagnola, he returned to Marradi where he wrote his first poems, heavily influenced by the 19th-century classical master, Carducci. In 1904, at the suggestion of a family friend who was the pharmacist in Marradi, he enrolled as a chemistry student at the University of Bologna. ("I studied chemistry by mistake and understood nothing about it. . . . I should have studied literature. If I had studied literature, I could have lived. Literature was a more balanced thing, the subject pleased me, I could have earned a living and straightened myself out. I didn't understand chemistry at all, and so I gave myself up to the void.")

Campana's restlessness sent him from school to school. In 1905 he was studying pharmaceutical chemistry in Florence. The next year, he took up the same subject in Bologna, and was also confined for the first time in an asylum, at Imola. The following year he travelled to Argentina, where he tried working at an incredible array of jobs: "I played the triangle in the Argentine Navy. I was a porter in Buenos Aires." He was also a "gaucho, a collier, a miner, a policeman, a gypsy, . . . a juggler, the manager of a rifle range, an accordian player . . . a stoker on commerical ships." In 1910, after returning to Marradi via Odessa, where he sold pinwheels in a fair, and Belgium, where he was jailed in Brussels and confined in a sanatorium at Tournai, he embarked on a pilgrimage to the ancient Franciscan monastery at La Verna, the subject of the journal that makes up a major part of the *Canti orfici*. He published a few poems in student magazines in Bologna in 1912, and, under the influence of futurism and Rimbaud, began to write the *Canti orfici* in Marradi.

The manuscript was finished in the fall of 1913, and in December Campana walked the forty miles to Florence, where he delivered his work to Giovanni Papini and Ardengo Soffici, editors of the influential futurist-oriented literary review *Lacerba*. Soffici lost the manuscript, however, and Campana was forced to reconstruct it from memory. He and a printer friend published it together in Marradi in 1914, with subtitle (in German) "The Tragedy of the Last German in Italy," and a dedication to "Wilhelm II, emperor of the Germans," which Campana told Soffici was aimed at the mindless patriotism of "those idiots in Marradi." He sold the book himself in the literary cafés, at the Paszkowski and the Giubbe Rosse in Florence and the San Pietro in Bologna. It was reported that he picked fights with other writers and tore out those pages of his book which he felt the purchaser was not worthy to receive, but Campana denied this to Binazzi: "A journalist's invention. If I sold the book it was because I was poor."

In 1915, after publishing his poem "Toscanità" in the famous review *Riviera ligure*, he went to work in Geneva, but was eventually returned home, and when he tried to enlist in the military, he was committed to a sanatorium. The pattern of alternating wandering and confinement continued, intensified. In the summer of 1916, he met and fell in love with the writer Sibilla Aleramo, author of the renowned feminist novel *Una donna* (*A Woman*), but their relationship lasted only a few months. Its demise seems to mark the end of Campana's attempt to live in the world.

Early in 1918, he was permanently admitted to the psychiatric hospital of Castel Pulci near Badia a Settimo, just west of Florence. Here, he wrote Binazzi ten years later, "I am very well off and I hope not to leave. . . . Who can say which among us all is crazy? But I am crazy! I have days of lucidity and days I cannot remember. I had a nervousness that was terribly profound and I couldn't live in any way. I was ill, certainly, exhausted in such a way that I was useless to society. . . . I live quietly. . . . I had some art but no longer do."

Campana died of septicemia at Castel Pulci on March 1, 1932. He was forty-six. He is buried in the church at Badia a Settimo.

Campana's critical fate in Italy, both during his lifetime and afterward, is discussed in Montale's 1942 essay about him, which appears at the back of this volume. My concern here is to try to say something about why this poetry is of interest today to readers from a very different tradition. What is there in Campana that comes across successfully into English?

To a reader who comes to Campana's work fresh it seems to me that what stands out above all is its helpless obsessiveness, its evasive centering on the sexual act and on the strangeness, the irreducible otherness of woman, seen not as another kind of human but as an almost monolithic fact of nature. There are no characters other than the perceiving "I" in Campana, only apparitions, figures, chimaeras, all of them female. "The Night" is the only poem which comes close to describing an actual encounter, with an "older woman" or "serving girl." Elsewhere, woman becomes a generalized metaphor for the dazzlingly enigmatic world: "the strong-smelling streets where women sang in the hot weather." The heat, the smell, the street, the women, their song — all are part of the otherness that Campana's poem is constantly trying to embrace and encompass (and perhaps extinguish) in a hymn of endlessly unfulfilled attraction:

> O woman I've dreamed over, woman adored, strong-minded woman, your profile ennobled by a memory of Byzantine stillness, noble and mythic head in strong, smooth lines gilded by the enigma of sphinxes: twilit eyes in a landscape of towers dreamed there on the banks of the war-torn plain, on the banks of rivers drunk

17

down by the savage earth there where
Francesca's cry is lost forever: from my
childhood a liturgical voice over and over
intoned in prayer slowly and movingly:
and you from that rhythm sacred to me and
much moved arose already restless with
vast plains, with distant miraculous desti-
nies: my hope reawakens on the endlessness
of the plain or the sea when I feel a breath
of grace flutter: nobility incarnate and
golden, golden depth of your eyes: hunt-
ress, lover, mystic, benign in human nobil-
ity ancient Romagna.

("La Verna")

Campana's is an atmosphere of heat and fire,
of ancient primordialness. Aspects of symbolist
painting come to mind — the eerie visionary
stillness of Redon, the sexual rapacity of
Khnopff, the atmospheric luminescence and
sense of enclosure of Moreau. Yet there is also a
sense of Mediterranean openness and nature, a
feeling of location which is missing in these
northern artists. Much as the world is Other,
Campana's native place in it is very strongly
felt. As with so many poets and artists of his cul-
ture, Campana's landscape is so much a part of

his understanding of his character that it comes to represent his own state of mind.

This deep rootedness, in a congenitally restless temperament like Campana's, may be one of the things that it is hardest for Americans to understand. Certainly his given vocabulary, the fund of imagery and experience on which he draws, is not familiar to us. The mythic, ancient, blood-ridden Mediterranean culture to which his title refers; the ascetic, penitential Catholicism of Andrea del Castagno and La Verna; the classic *toscanità* or Tuscanness that is Campana's ground and heritage, "bare and elegant, simple and austere" — all of this we can at best appreciate rationally, not feel. Campana's understanding of the ancientness of his place and culture is something no non-European can fathom about Europe. Yet the strangeness at the heart of this strangeness, the sense of personal isolation, of sexual need, of physical and metaphysical displacement, are deeply familiar. They have affinities with what we can feel in different, perhaps less desperate form in the work of Rimbaud and Eliot, Kafka and Montale, Celan and Artaud.

Campana's portrayal of himself as a lone traveler in a land of eerie Leonardine lakes and caves and De Chirican squares, his "mystic nightmare of chaos," his sense of himself as both Orphic priest-perpetrator and Orphic/Christian victim[3] — is a distilled, intensified version of modern existential anxiousness. And his artfully raw and eerily beautiful presentation of his dislocation answers to our psychologically overeducated, even prurient hunger for "real" data, for the pure, unadulterated, uncleaned-up expression of feeling.

Campana's vision is extreme in a way that we have come to identify as authentic. The ecstatic pressure of his language, its relentless, manic lyricism, its violent beauty, its verging on incoherence, are the essence of its attraction for a readership that has only really begun to absorb the "de-civilizing" displacement that European modernism, and surrealism in particular, has wreaked on the empirical Anglo-American tradition. Yet unlike so much in this new tradition (including the futurism he rejected) Campana's work has the force of necessity behind it. Its strangeness is truly, irreducibly strange.

Campana's obscurity, when he is obscure, is in homage to his own peculiar perception of what surrounds him. It is impossible for him to "understand" and thus codify and de-nature the

Other. Instead, naked and alone, he confronts the irreducible difference, the final unknowability, of what is out there. And we, from within the thin protective shell of our constructed culture, respond with amazement to his courage in facing and identifying what seems, on closer inspection, to be some previously hidden part of ourselves.

1. In the introduction to his translation of Campana, *Orphic Songs* (New York: October House, 1968).

2. This remark and all quotations from Campana himself are drawn from the biographical note by Enrico Falqui in the 1966 edition of the *Canti orfici e altri scritti* (Firenze: Vallecchi).

3. The *Canti orfici* end with this misquotation from Whitman's *Song of Myself:* "They were all torn and cover'd with the boy's blood."

THE NIGHT

I

The Night

I remember an old city, red walls and red battlements, on the immense plain burnt out from the August heat, with the far-away spongy cold comfort of green hills in the background. Enormous emptiness of bridge-arches over the stagnant river dried to thin leaden puddles: a black moulding of gypsies shifting and silent along the banks: among the dazzle and glare of a distant cane-brake the far-off naked figures of teen-age boys and the Hasidic beard of an old man: and suddenly out of the midst of the dead water the gypsy women came and a song, primordial dirge from the voiceless swamp monotonous and irritating: and time ground down and held still.

*

I raised my eyes unconsciously to the barbarous tower which dominated the long avenue of plane trees. Above a silence wound to intensity it began to drag from the dead its distant savage mythology: at the same time, through other distant hallucinations, other vague, violent apprehensions, another myth — also mysterious and wild —kept coming back to me. Down below the old women, the strollers, had dragged their long dresses softly toward the vague splendor of the gate: the countryside was beginning to numb up and go sleepy in its network of canals; young girls with weightless hair, and profiles cut from medallions, disappeared now and then in little carts around green bends in the road. The sweet silver toll of a bell from far away: Evening: in the empty chapel, in the shadows of the modest nave, I held Her, the rose-pale flesh and the burning fugitive eyes: years and years and years melted together in the triumphal sweet taste of the memory.

*

The person I once had been found himself unconsciously heading toward the barbarous tower, legendary keeper of adolescent dreams. In the silence of ancient lanes and half-streets he climbed up alongside the church and the convent walls: you couldn't even hear the noise of his footsteps. A deserted little piazza, broken hovels like old bruises, dead windows: to one side in an enormous wash of light, the tower, eight-pointed arid impenetrably red and unadorned; a dried-up 16th-century fountain kept silent, its stone shattered in the middle of its own Latin commentary. A deserted cobblestone road opened up toward the city.

*

He was startled by a door that had been thrown open. Old men, crooked and silent bony forms, straddled and crawled over each other with their piercing elbows, terrible in the wide light. Then they stopped with anxious and servile bows in front of the whiskery face of a monk who was leaning out from the emptiness of a doorway, and then slinked away muttering, raising themselves up little by little, dragging their long shadows after them one by one across the red and flaking walls, each one just like a shadow. A woman with a swinging walk and a foolish laugh joined them, finishing off the cortege.

*

They stretched their shadows out along the red plaster-flaked walls: he followed, an automaton. He said one word to the woman and it fell into the noon silence: an old man turned to stare at him with an absurd vacant and luminous look. And the woman kept on smiling with a soft sweet smile in the aridity of noon, doltish and alone in the catastrophic light.

*

I never knew how I saw my own shadow coasting along the torpid canals, my ghost that laughed back at me from the depths. It went with me along the strong-smelling streets where women sang in the hot weather. At the edge of the countryside a door cut in the stone, watched by a young woman in a red dress, pale and fat, caught its eye: I entered. An aging but opulent older woman was sitting inside, profile like a ram's, with black hair twisted loosely about her sculptural head wildly decorated by a rheumy eye like a black gem stone with bizarre facets, agitated by childish graces that kept resurfacing like false hopes being pulled from a deck of cards in long sanctimonious strange theories of languishing queens a king infantrymen weapons and knights. I spoke to her and a voice from the convent, deep and melodramatic answered me along with a wrinkled and gracious smile. I could see stretched out in the shadows the maidservant half nude who slept with her mouth half open, her throat rattling in a heavy sleep, her beautiful body supple and amber. I sat down slowly.

*

The long thread of speculations about her loves unravelled monotonously in my ears. Old family portraits were scattered sanctimoniously over the table. The lithe figure with amber skin stretched out on a bed and listened curiously, leaning on her elbow like a sphinx: outside the green green orchard between reddened walls: only we three alive in the southern hush.

*

In the meantime the sun had set and had wound up in its gold, as a spider winds up its prey, the buzzing center of memory and seemed to consecrate it. The voice of the Procuress became sweeter little by little, and her head like that of an oriental priestess seemed comfortable in languid poses. The black magic of evening, sly girlfriend of the criminal, was the go-between for our dark souls and its splendors seemed to promise a mysterious reign. And the priestess of sterile pleasures, the ingenuous and greedy maidservant and the poet all watched each other, barren souls unwittingly looking for the problem of their lives. But the evening only sent down a golden message from the fresh shudderings of the night.

*

Night came, and the conquest of the serving girl. Her amber body her voracious mouth her bristling black hair at times the revelation of lust in her terrified eyes wove and rewove a fantastic situation. Sweeter meanwhile, and already just about to die out, the memory still reigned in the distance of the persuasive older woman, still queen in her classic line among the great sisters of memory: after Michelangelo had bent her down again on her tired knees tired from her journey she who bends, who bends but will not lie down, barbarous queen under the weight of the whole human dream, and the battering of arcane and violent poses of the overthrown queens of antiquity who heard Dante extinguish himself in Francesca's cry there on the banks of rivers which exhausted from wars open their mouths, while on their own banks love's everlasting pain is recreated. And the serving girl, the ingenuous Magdalene of the bristly hair and brilliant eyes, was begging with tremors of her barren, golden body, crude and savage, sweetly closed in the humility of her mystery. The long night full of the deceits of various images.

*

The old images appeared at the silver gates of the first adventures, sweetened by a life of love, to protect me again with their smiles of ineffable mystery and tenderness. The closed halls were opened where light falls in a steady sheet to infinity in the mirrors, random images of courtesans appearing in their sphinx-like posturings out of the reflected pale light: and once more everything that had been arid and sweet, the unpetalled roses of youth, returned to full bloom on the skeletal panorama of the world.

*

In the gunpowder smell of festival night, the last clanging dying away down the air, I saw the young girls of antiquity, those of the first illusion, appear clearly in the middle of the bridges that jut out from the city to the suburb in the torrid summer nights: faces turned to a three-quarters view, listening to the insistent clanging from the suburb announcing the tongues of fire in uneasy lamps boring through a night sky already full of orgiastic lights: now sweetened: in the already-dead and rose-blushed sky, unburdened by the veil of light: thus Saint Marta, instruments broken on the ground, the song already hushed across the ever-green landscapes that the heart of Saint Cecilia tunes with the Latin sky, soft and pink near the old twilight resting in the heroic line of great Roman women. Memories of gypsies, memories of long-ago loves, memories of music and light: exhaustions of love, sudden exhaustions on a pensione bed long ago, another adventurous cradle of uncertainty and regret: thus all that was once more sterile and sweet, the roses of youth unpetalled and dry, sprang up on the skeletal panorama of the world.

*

In the evening of flamebursts from the summer festival, in a white and delicious light, when our ears just barely rested in the silence and our eyes were tired from the garlands of fireworks, from the multicolored stars that left an acrid smell of gunpowder, a beautiful reddish weight everywhere in the air, walking side by side made us weary exalting in our own too-diverse beauty, she thin and delicate and dark, pure of eye and face, the dazzle of the necklace lost on her bare throat, walking now with hesitant steps clutching a fan. She was attracted to the hut: her white gown undulated in thin blue jerks through the diffuse light and I followed the pallor burning her forehead under her dark bangs. We went in. Dark, autocratic faces, serene again in the illusion of childhood and the festival, turned toward us, profoundly clear in the light. And we watched the scene, everything a spectral unreality. There were skeletal overviews of the city.

Bizarre dead bodies looked up at the sky in stiff postures. A rubber odalisque breathed in a low voice and turned her idol's eyes around the room. And the sharp smell of sawdust that muted footsteps and the continual tide-like whispering of the young women of the town astonished at the mystery. "Is it Paris, then? There's London. The Battle of Mukden." We looked around: it must have been late. All those things seen through the magnetic eyes of the lenses in that dream light! Motionless next to me I felt her grow strange and withdrawn while her fascination deepened under the dark bangs of her hair. She moved. And I felt with a bitter twinge which was immediately consoled that I would never be near her again. I followed her then as you follow a dream you love in vain: thus we had become suddenly far apart and strangers to each other after the tumult of the festival, in front of the skeletal panorama of the world.

*

I was in the shadow of an arcade which dripped drop after drop of blood-gorged light through the fog of a December night. Without warning a door was flung open in a splendor of light. In the foreground of the far end of the room in the luminescence of a red ottoman an older woman was lying up on one elbow, her head resting in her hand, her brown eyes like brown fire, her breasts enormous: beside her a young girl on her knees, amber and thin, hair cut into bangs down her forehead, a youthful grace, her legs smooth and uncovered beneath her shimmering gown: and over her, over the serious thoughtful older woman with young eyes a curtain, a white lace curtain, a curtain that seemed to move images, the images above her, the pure clean images over the thoughtful older woman with young eyes. Beaten by light from the shadows of the arcade gorged drops of blood-light falling over and over I stared compelled and amazed at the symbolic and daring grace of the scene. It was already late, we were alone and between us an unfettered intimacy was born and the older woman with the young eyes who lay at the far end of the room under the moving white lace curtain talked to me. Her life was a long sin: lust. Lust but still full of an unsatisfiable curiosity for her. "The female peppered him with kisses from the right side: why from the right? Later the male pigeon stayed overhead, immobile?, ten minutes. Why?" The questions remained unanswered, as pushed by nostalgia she remembered her past over and over again. Until the conversation languished and the voice had died out around us, the mystery of sensuality having reclothed whomever it had reinvoked. Upset, tears blearing my eyes in front of the white lace curtain I kept on following the white fantasies. The voice had gone silent around us. Then she had gone. The voice had gone silent. Certainly I had heard her brushing past in destroying silence. In front of the curtain of crumpled lace the young girl was still resting on her amber knees, bending bending with the grace of an acolyte to love.

*

Faust was young and handsome and had curly hair. Women from Bologna at that time resembled Siracusean medallions and the slant of their eyes was so perfect that they loved to appear immobile in order to contrast harmoniously with their long brown curls. It was easy to run into them at night in the dark streets (when the moon lit up the streets) and Faust would raise his eyes to the gables of the houses which looked in the moonlight like question marks and then would stare pensively at the diminishing trail of the girls' footsteps. From the old tavern where the students gathered he sometimes liked to hear among the calm talk of the Bologna winter, cold and foggy like his own, and the snap and crack of the wooden logs and the dart and flash of the flames on the ochre vaults and sometimes the hurried footsteps under the near arches. He loved then to gather himself in song while the young waitress in her red petticoats, and with her beautiful cheeks under her smoky hair-do walked back and forth in front of him. Faust was young and handsome. On a morning like that, from the little wall-papered room, among refrains from the player piano and a floral arrangement, from the little room I had heard the crowd rush by and the dark noises of winter. O I remember!: I was young, my hand never just quietly holding up my indecisive face, kind from anxiety and exhaustion. In those days I unburdened myself to the polished, supple dressmaker's dummies, consecrated by my anxiety about supreme love, by the anxiety of all my tormented and thirsty childhood. Everything was mysterious to my faith, my life was entirely "an anxiety about the secret of the stars, everything a bowing over the abyss." I was handsome with torment, restless pale thirsting wandering behind the ghosts of that mystery. Then I fled. I lost myself in the tumult of the colossal cities, saw white cathedrals raise themselves in enormous congeries of faith and dreams with their thousand spires in the air, I saw the Alps raise themselves like still grander cathedrals, and full of the great green shadows of firs, and full of the melody of their rivers and streams in which I heard the song born from the everlastingness of dreams. Up there among the smoky firs in the fog, among their thousand tickings the thousand voices of silence a small light came clear among the tree trunks, and I started up on that path of light: I climbed up to the Alps, into the delicate white mysterious backdrop of the countryside. Lakes, up there among the luminous rocks ponds watched over by the dream's smile, luminous pools the lakes ecstatic from the oblivion that you, Leonardo, dissembled. The stream told me the story vaguely. I stood still among the immobile lances of the firs believing at times I was bringing forth a new melody wild and yet sad perhaps fixing for good the clouds which seemed to slow down curiously for a moment on that bottomless landscape spy on it and then vanish behind the immobile lances of the fir trees. And poor, naked, happy to be poor and naked, to reflect for an instant the landscape like a memory fascinating and horrible deep in my heart I was climbing: and I got there got up there where the Alpine snows blocked my path for good. A young girl was washing in the stream, washing and singing in the white snows of the Alps. She turned, welcomed me, and in the night she loved me. And still in the background the Alps the white delicate mystery, lit the purity of the stellar lamp in my memory, and the light of love's night burned on.

*

But which nightmare still weighed all my youth down? O the kisses the vain kisses of the young girl washing, washing and singing in the white snows of the Alps! (tears came to my eyes with her memory). I heard the still-distant stream: it poured down soaking ancient and desolate cities, streets long silent, empty as after a pillaging. A golden warmth in the shadow of the present room, a lavish head of hair a death-rattling nightmarish body in the mystic night of the age-old human animal. The handmaiden was sleep-

ing the oblivion of her own dark dreams: like a
Byzantine icon, like an Arabian myth the uncer-
tain pallor of the curtain whitened the back-
ground.

*

And then fictions of a very old and free life, of
enormous solar myths and massacres that created
themselves before my spirit. I saw an old image
again, a skeletal form alive because of the great
force of a barbarous myth, eyes abyss-like and
changing glaring with dark blood, in the dream's
torture discovering the vulcanized body, two
spots two bullet holes on her extinct breasts. I
thought I heard the guitars shudder over there in
the board-and-branch shack on the lonely fields
of the city, a candle throwing light on the bare
ground. In front of me a wild older woman
stared me down without batting an eyelash. The
light was weak on the bare ground in the quiver-
ing of the guitars. To one side on the blossoming
treasure of a young dreaming girl the woman
now clung like a spider while seeming to
whisper words in my ear I couldn't make out,
words sweet as the wordless wind of the Pampas
that sinks you. The wild woman had grabbed
me: my indifferent blood had certainly been

drunk by the earth: and now the light was even weaker on the bare ground under the metallic breath of the guitars. Suddenly the freed young girl breathed out her childhood, her eyes as soft and piercing as the abyss, languid in her wild grace. And grace grew weaker on the back of the beautiful young thing the shadow of her watery hair and the august mane of the tree of life weaving itself into the ending on the bare ground the guitars inviting a distant sleep. One could hear clearly a leap of wild horses from the Pampas a pawing in the earth, could hear clearly the wind rise, the pawing seeming to be drowned out in the roar of infinity. In the square of the open door the stars flashed brilliantly red and hot in the distance: the shadow of the wild ones in shadow.

II

The Voyage and Return

Voices rose, and other voices, and children's songs and songs of lust, through the twisted little streets inside the burning shadow, to the hill to the hill. In the shadow of the green lamps the white colossal prostitutes dreamed dreams of longing in a light made fantastic by the wind. The sea poured out its salt into the wind which the wind mixed and washed in the lust-smell of the alleys, and the white Mediterranean night joked with the huge shapes of the women while the flame's bizarre death-attempts went on and on in the streetlamp's cave. They watched the flame and sang songs about hearts in chains. All the preludes were quieted now. The night, the stillest joy of the night had fallen. The Moorish doors loaded up and twisted themselves with monstrous black wonders while, in the distance the dark blue dredged a small harbor of stars. Lonely the night now sat on her throne bedizened and fired with all her swarm of stars and flame. In front like a monstrous wound a street deepened. At the sides of the door's angle, white caryatids of a false heaven dreamed away their faces resting on the palms of their hands. She had the pure imperial line in her profile and her throat was bound about with the splendor of opals. With the quick imperial gesture of youth she drew her light dress in one movement over her shoulders and her window shimmered in expectation until shadows closed it softly into a double shadow. And my heart was starved for dreams, for her, for the evanescent one like evanescent love, the love-donor of the doors, caryatid of destiny's heaven. On her divine knees, on her body pale as a dream come forth from the innumerable dreams of the shadows, among the innumerable deceiving lights, the ancient friend, the eternal Chimera held in her red hands my red and ancient heart.

*

Return. In the room where I had embraced her shapes revealed by the curtains of light, a lingering breath: and in the twilight my unsullied lamp stars my heart longing for memories again. Faces, faces whose eyes laughed in the just-blooming dreamflower, you young charioteers on the weightless dreamstreets you garlanded so zealously: O fragile poems, O garland of night-loves . . . A song breaks from the garden like the weak link in a chain of sobs: the vein is open: dry and red and sweet is the skeletal panorama of the world.

*

O your body! Your perfume veiled my eyes: I

41

didn't see your body (a sweet and acute perfume): there in the great empty mirror, in the great empty mirror veiled by violet smoke, at the top, kissed by a star of light was the beautiful, the beautiful and sweet gift of a god: and the timid breasts were stuffed with light, and the stars were absent, and there wasn't a God in the night of violet love: but you light as down you sat on my knees, night-breathing caryatid of an enchanted heaven. Your body an airy gift on my knee, and the stars in hiding, and there was no God in the night of violet love: but you in the night of violet love: but you with your violet eyes lowered, you from an unknown night sky which had already ravished one melody of caresses. I remember, love: light as a dove's wings you rested your limbs on my own noble limbs. They breathed happily, inhaling their own beauty, my limbs breathing a clearer light in your obedient cloud of divine reflections. O don't burn them! don't burn them! Don't burn them: all is vanity vain is the dream: all is in vain all is dream: Love, spring of the dream you are alone you are alone who appears in the veil of violet smoke. Like a white cloud, like a white cloud next to my heart, O stay O stay O stay. Don't sadden O sun!

We opened the window to the night sky. Men like wandering spirits: they wandered like ghosts: and the city (the streets the churches the squares), composed itself in a cadenced dream, as if through an invisible melody sprung from that wandering. Therefore wasn't the world inhabited by sweet spirits and wasn't the dream awakened again in the night in all its triumphant powers? Which bridge, we asked silently, which bridge have we thrown across to the infinite, so that everything appears to us as a shadow of eternity? To which dream have we raised the nostalgia of our beauty? The moon rose in her old robe behind the Byzantine church.

III

The End

In the pleasant warmth of the red light, inside those closed rooms where light sinks flat inside the mirrors to infinity the whiteness of lace blooms then withers away. The concierge in the cast-off luxury of a green jerkin, the lines of her face kinder, her eyes which in their brightness hide the dark watches the silver door. You feel the indefinite fascination of love. A mature woman is in control sweetened by a life of love a smile on her face a lovely glimmer in her eyes the memory of the flashing tears of sensuality. They pass during her vigil, rich with messengers of love, light spools weaving multicolored fantasies, they wander about, luminous dust that rests in the enigma of mirrors. The concierge watches the silver door. Outside is the night leafy with silent songs, pale love of the wanderers.

CHIMERA

I don't know if your white face appeared to me
Among the rocks, or if you were
Some smile from the unknown distances,
Your ivory forehead slanted to brilliance
Young sister of Mona Lisa:
O fired springs,
For your legendary whiteness
O Queen O adolescent Queen:
But for your unknown poem
Of lust and sorrow
Music bloodless daughter
Marked by a line of blood
In the pouty circle of your lips,
Queen of melody:

But for your virgin head
Inclining, I poet of the night
Watched the stars in the sky's deeps,
I for your sweet mystery
I for your turning silence.
And don't know if the pale flame
Of your hair was the living sign
Of its bloodlessness,
And don't know if it was a sweet vapor,
Sweet on my own sorrow,
Smile of a night face:
I look at the white rocks the dumb fountains of
    wind
And the unmovableness of the firmaments
And the swollen rivers that go on weeping
And the shadows of workers curved there on the
    cold hills
And still through the soft and far-away skies
    clear shadows running
And still I call you and still I call you Chimera.

AUTUMN GARDEN

(Florence)

To the spectral garden to the silent laurel
Of green garlands
To the autumnal earth
A last goodbye!
To the hard dry hillsides
Reddened in the hand-heavy sun
A confusion of raw noises
From life far away:
It cries to the setting sun
That bloodies the flower beds in its going down.

You hear the fanfare
That rises like a rip in the old fabric: the river
     disappears
In the gold sands: in the silence
The white statues on top of the bridgeheads
Have turned: and things that once were are no
     longer so.
And from down below like a chorus
Soft and majestic
Silence rises and gasps to the height of my
     balcony:
And in the smell of laurel,
In the sharp and persistent laurel smell,
Among the immortal statues against the sunset
She appears to me, here and present.

SONG OF DARKNESS

Light in the twilight begins to thin:
Fidgety ghosts may darkness be sweet
To the heart that has stopped loving!
Sources watery sources we have to listen,
Sources sources that know
Sources that know that ghosts from below
That ghosts are here to listen . . .
Listen: light in the twilight is thinning out
And to the fidgety ghosts darkness is sweet:
Listen: Bad Luck has tapped you out:
But for the released hearts another life is at the
        door:

There is no sweetness that can equal Death
Never Never Never
Understand who still rocks your cradle:
Understand the sweet lips that ladle
This oil in your ear: Never Never
And here the wind rises and packs up:
And here it comes back in its cup
From the sea and here is the gulp
We hear the heart make that loved us forever!
Let's see: already the landscape
Of trees and waters has grown dark
The speechless river looks hard as bark . . .
Bam! Mama, that man up there in the weather!

LA VERNA

I
La Verna (diary)

15 September (on the road to Campigno)

Three girls and a donkey on the mule track coming down the mountain. Complimentary wisecracks from the road workers. The donkey who rolls in the dirt. Laughter. Mountain profanities. The rocks and the river.

. . . .
Castagno, 17 September

The Falterona is still wrapped in fog. I can only see rocky runoffs that vein its sides, then lose themselves in a fog-sky which alternating waves of sunlight fail to thin out. Rain has made the grey mountain a slick darkness. In front of the fountain the people of Castagno have been sitting a long time now waiting for the sun, weighed down by the long night of rain in their flooded hovels. A girl in broken shoes walks by saying submissively, 'one day the flooding will carry us all away.' The swollen stream in its dark noise remarks on all this misery. I look on oppressed at the steep rocks of the Falterona: I will have to climb, and climb. In the presbytery I find a tablet to Andrea del Castagno. The type of the local girls suddenly strikes me: wooden face, deepset dark eyes, cave-like dark tones on faded yellowish tones: contrasted with such a simple antique Tuscan grace in the profile and neck as to render them quite pleasant! perhaps. How different the evening at Campigno: how mystical its landscape, how beautiful the poverty of its hovels! How enchantingly the stars rose for me in the sky and how fateful: against the distant backdrop of the web of valleys the barbarous valley disappeared in, the same mist the restless stream came out of dark with meaning! I felt the stars flow up and settle back luminously on that mystery. Raising my eyes to the highest peak of the rock mountain cut in a toothy semicircle onto the violet twilight, solitary and magnificent arc strained to the breaking point by catastrophe under the restless piling up of rocks out to the ambush of the infinite, I was not ravished I was not ravished to discover lights more lights in the sky. And, while time was disappearing in vain for me, a song, the long waves of a triple chorus rising then flung out from the rocks, restrained at last on the golden borders of night by their own echo which sunk them again into the strong breast of the landscape pushing them back and away, lost forever.

The song was brief: a pause, a sudden and mysterious comment, and the mountain again took on its catastrophic dream. The brief song: the three young girls had expressed desperately, in a millenary cadenza, their brief, dark pain and were then silenced in the night. All the windows in the valley were lit up. I was alone.

The fog has lifted: I go out. The good, homey smell of lavender and washing that small Tuscan villages have makes me happy again. The church has a portico of small squared columns made of whole stones, bare and elegant, simple and austere, truly Tuscan. Among the cypresses I notice other porticos. On one hillside a cross opens its arms to the vast flanks of the Falterona, dark booty, which in turn lays bare its own rocky structure. The grasses burn in the graveyard with a pale red-ochre flame.

— On the Falterona (Giogo)

The Falterona green black and silver: the formal sadness of the Falterona that swells up like an enormous petrified breaker, that leaves behind a cavalry of cracks and splits and chinks in the rock down to the sandy boiling up again of hills there on the Tuscan plain: Castagno, little stone houses scattered about half-way up the mountain, windows I saw lit up: thus to the creatures of this cubist landscape, in a light barely gilded by the inner eye among thin vegetable-like hairs the rectangle of the head in a line occulty fine out of the delicate features the smile of the blonde Ceres shows through: the clear grey eyes limpid under the black line of the eyebrow: sweetness of the lip line, serenity of the eyebrow memory of the Tuscan poetry that once was.

(You had already understood O Leonardo, O divine primitive!)

— Campigna, forest of the Falterona

(The quadrangular houses made out of living stone by the Lorenas remain empty, and the avenue of linden trees gives a romantic overtone to the solitude where the mighty of the earth have built their homes. Evening slides down from the Alpine crest and collects itself in the green bosom of the spruce trees.)

From the avenue of linden trees I watched a solitary star catch fire on the Alpine spur of rock and the ancient forest shadows coagulate and the deep-ditched rustlings of silence. From the sharp peak in the sky, over the drowsy mystery of the forest going down the avenue of lindens I spotted my old friend the moon who rose up in a new red dress of coppery smoke: and I greeted my friend again without surprise as though the savage depths of the crag were waiting for her to surge up out of the unknown landscape. Meanwhile I went on down the avenue of lindens protected from all enchantments while you rose and disappeared my sweet friend moon, a solitary and smoky vapor over the barbaric clefts and slices. And I didn't look up again at your strange face but wanted to keep on walking a long time down the avenue if I had heard your red aurora in the breathing of the night life of the forest.

Stia, 20 September

In the hotel an old Milanese gentleman talks of his distant love affairs to a white-haired lady who has a face like a baby's. Calmly she explains the vagaries of the heart to him: he is still amazed and becomes distressed: here in this old village enclosed in the woods. I have left Castagno: I climbed the Falterona slowly following the course of the fast-flowing stream: I rested in the angelic purity of the high mountain glazed over and brilliant from dark shadings left from the recent rains, sparkling against the sky in the clear and luminous contours that once made me dream standing in front of the hills in old paintings. I stopped in the houses of Campigna. I went down interminable valleys wild and deserted seeing the sudden background of a promised landscape, a distant and isolated castle: and at the end Stia, white and elegant among the greenery, melodious with her serene castles: the first greeting of happy life in a new town: the poetry of Tuscany still alive in the piazza sonorous with tranquil voices, watched over by the old castle: the ladies on their balconies leaning their pure profiles languidly in the evening: the

hour of grace in the day, of rest and forget-
fulness.

Outside all is quiet: the brotherly conversation
of the gentleman continues:

> Comme deux ennemis rompus
> Que leur haine ne soutient plus
> Et qui laissent tomber leurs armes!

21 September (near La Verna)

I saw a turtle dove break off from the mystical
solitudes and glide toward the open immensity
of the valleys. The Christian landscape marked
by crosses bent over by the wind was myste-
riously quickened by it. The dove glided end-
lessly on its outstretched locked wings, light as
a little boat on the ocean. Goodbye, dove, O
goodbye! The soaring rock columns of La Verna
rose up into peaks grey in the twilight, all ringed
around by the dark forest.

The hospitality of the local peasants was en-
chantingly Christian. I was covered with sweat
and they offered me water. "You will arrive at
La Verna within an hour if God wishes it." A
little girl watched me a bit sadly I thought, her

black eyes amazed under an enormous straw hat. In all an unconscious absorption and a convent-like serenity sweetened each feature of their faces. I'll remember the little girl for a long time and her tranquil know-everything eyes under her nunnish hat.

Higher up on the interminable stubble always higher the natural rock towers rose up and up supporting the little house that looked like a convent its windows lit and relit by rays of the setting sun.

The fortress of the spirit was rising, enormous rocks thrown in heaps and piles by a violent law toward the sky, then soothed by nature before it had covered them with green forests, soothed later still by an infinite spirit of love: the purpose which had soothed over the jarring blows of the ideal that had tortured it, and to which they were the sacred pure and supreme emotions of my life.

22 September (La Verna)

"Francesca B. O divine St Francis pray for me poor sinner. 20 August 189 . . ."

I had gone through the forest remembering something that made me feel my first traumatic anxiety again. I kept remembering the victorious eyes, the line of the eyebrows: perhaps she'd never known about it: and now I found her at the end of my pilgrimage that broke out in a confession so sweet, up there and so far away from everything. It was written halfway down the corridor where the Via Crucis branches out from the life of St Francis: (through the gratings the frozen breath rises from the grottoes below). Halfway down, in front of the simple figure of love her heart had opened into a cry into a tear of passion, and destiny had been perfected.

Deep grottoes, rocky fissures where stone steps went down down into unremembering shadow, colossal steeps and bas-reliefs of columns cut in the living rock: and in the church the angel, sweet purity that the lily shares and the Virgin elects, and a fluffy cloud turns blue in the sky and a classical amphora encloses the earth and the lilies: who appears in the proper foreshortening the one the dream appears in, and in the white cloud of her beauty rests an instant knee on the earth up there like that next to heaven:

. . . .

solitary little streets among the tall columnars of trees, content with a slight ray of sun . . . . until I arrived there, in front of the veiled immensity of the landscape where a divine nocturnal sweetness revealed itself to me in the morning, the green completely covered with a bright shine which shaded over and slowly diminished out to infinity: still full of the power of its chains outlined against the lingering darkness. Caprese, Michelangiolo, she whom you bent over on her knees so tired of walking, who bends and bends and never rests, in her arcane pose so like the ancient sisters, like the ancient barbarous queens hurling forever in the whirlwind of Dante's song, barbarous queen under the whole weight of the human dream . . . .

. . . .

The corridor, filled with the iced breath from the caves, is covered completely with the Franciscan legend. The saint appears as the shadow of Christ, resigned, born in the land of Humanism, who accepts his destiny in solitude. His renunciation is simple and sweet: from his loneliness he chants his hymn to nature with great faith and fidelity: Brother Sun, Sister Water, Brother Wolf. A beloved Italian saint. Now they have redone his chapel carved out of the living rock. A walnut tableau runs completely around it where with melancholic power a monk . . . from Bibbiena inlaid half-figures of saintly monks. The bizarre simplicity of the white design is raised up time and again when the golden light of sunset tries to spill over from the close glass window into the penumbra of the chapel. Those simple designs then take on a bizarre and nostalgic fascination. White on the rich walnut surfaces seems to elevate the hieratic profiles of the slight claustral landscape they rise from beheaded, figures of a saintliness made wholly spirit, the enigmatic and rigid lines of great unknown souls. A decrepit monk drags himself in the late hour through the half-light in front of the altar, silent in his shaggy robe, and prays the prayers of 80 years of devotion. Outside the sunset muddies and darkens. Threatening iron-colored streaks lower and weigh down on the mountains facing us in the distance. The dream approaches its end and the spirit suddenly alone seeks out a support some faith in the sad hour. Far off one sees the mysterious lookouts and warriors of the Casentino castles slowly go under. All around us a vast silence stretches out a vast emptiness in the false light from the cold glitterings still flickering under the pressure of darkness. And my memory suddenly flashes back to the gentle ladies with white arms down there on their balconies: as though in a dream: as though in a chivalrous dream.

I go out: the main piazza is deserted. I sit on the low wall. Figures wander by, and the dim lights vamp and go out: the monks take leave of the pilgrims. A breath of wind continuous and soft blows down from the wood above, but one hears neither its rustling on the dark mountainside nor its flow through the grottoes. A bell from the little Franciscan church tolls through the sadness of the monastery: and it seems like the day of the great shade, the day in tears that it is dying.

II
Return

I LEAP (into space, out of time)

Water wind
The purity of first things —
Man's work on the element
Of water — nature that blankets

Layers of rock on top of layers — the wind
That plays around in the valleys — and the
    shadow of wind
The cloud — the far-off admonition
Of the river in the valley —
And the ruin of the mountain's spur — the
    landslide
Victory of the elements — the wind
That plays around in the valley.
Up the long valley that rises in terraces
The little stone house in the exhausted greenery:
The white image of the element.

The Telluric melody of the Falterona. Telluric
waves. The last asterisk of the Falterona's song
gets lost in the clouds. On the distant hillside the
triumphant line of young firs glistens, the ad-
vance guard of young giants grouped together
for battle, radiant in the sunlight strung out
along the long torrential slope. Behind them, in
the rustling of the black woods extending their
encampments farther and farther down the val-
ley the enormous rock folds and turns in on itself
grotesquely, like a pachyderm with four hooves
under its dark huge body: La Verna. I cross and I
go across it.

Campigno: barbarous country, always vanishing, night country, mystic nightmare of chaos. Your one inhabitant offers up the true night of the ancient human animal in all its gestures. In your troubled mountains the element of the grotesque is outlined: a lout and a fat whore flee under the flying clouds. And your white sides like the clouds, triangular, curved like full sails: barbarous country, vanishing always, night country, mystic nightmare of chaos.

. . . .

I'm resting now for the last time in the solitude of the forest. Dante, his poetry of ascendence, comes back whole in my memory. O pilgrim, O pilgrims who go out searching so seriously. Catherine, bizarre daughter of the barbarous mountain, of the rocky shell of the winds, how sweet is your weeping: how sweet it is when you were present at the painful scene of the mother, the mother who now had her last son dead. One of the pious women around her, kneeling tried to console her: but she didn't want to be consoled, but she who had thrown herself to the ground wanted to cry out all her grief. Figure out of Ghirlandaio, last daughter of the Tuscan poetry that once was, you got down then from your horse you then were watching: you who arose in the overflowing waves of your own hair, arose with your own company, as in the ancient poetic fables: already having forgotten the love of the poet.

Monte Filetto, 25 September

A nightingale sings in the limbs of the walnut tree. The hill is too beautiful against the too-blue sky. The river sings its own sweet selfsame song as best it can. It's been an hour now that I've watched the space below and the road halfway up the hill that leads there. Up here the hawks live. The fine summer rain patterned a fine tune on the walnut leaves. But the leaves of the acacia tree dear to the night submitted without a sound like a green shadow. The blue opens up between these two trees. The walnut stands in front of my room's window. At night it seems to gather all of the darkness up and curve its shadowy melody of leaves like a harvest of songs about its milky round and almost human trunk: the acacia knows how to outline itself like an illusion of smoke. The stars were pirouetting on the deserted hilltop. No one is coming down the street. I like to watch the empty countryside with its scattered trees from my balcony, the soul of solitude beaten out by the wind. Today when the wind and the whole landscape were so sweet after the rain I thought of the young ladies in de Maupassant and Jammes their pale oval faces inclined over the tapestries and engravings full of memories. The river takes up its lullaby again. I walk away. I look back at the window once more: the slope is a little golden painting among the quick cries of the hawks.

Near Campigno (26 September)

To render the landscape, virgin country that only the tame river in the valley fills with noises of a quivering freshness, painting would never be enough, you need water, the element itself, the tractable melody of water that spreads out among the draws and ravines from the ample gorge of its own bed, that sweet as the ancient voices of the wind presses down the valleys in regal curves: because here she is truly queen of the landscape.

. . . .

Valdervé is a hillside entirely Alpine which drops down suddenly over the crags and ravines and buries its pedestal in the water like the fang of a lion. The water turns here with clear deep thrashing sounds leaving the high pastoral scenery with its great trees and hills.

. . . .

Here are the rocks, strata upon strata, monuments of that solitary tenacity which console the anxious hearts of all men. And my destiny seemed sweet to me fleeing towards the far-spangled illusory fascinations that still stream down from the blue mountains: and to hear the susurration of waters under the bare-faced rocks, still breathfresh from the depths of the earth. Thus I know a music sweet in my memory and never remember one note of it: I know that it's called Departure or Return: I know a painting lost among the splendor of Florentine art with its message of sweet nostalgia: it's the prodigal son under the shade trees of his father's house. Literature? I don't know. My memory, water is like this. After the spiritual backdrops that have no spirit, after the beaten gold of twilight, sweet as the song of encompassing darkness is the song of water under the rocks: the way the essence is sweet in the black splendor of the eyes of Spanish virgins: and the chords of Spanish guitars . . . Ribera, where did I see your dances like bitter songs? Your whip-flick satire about the dance of victorious songs? And against your other face, the horseman of death, your other face that is the heart's deep core, the heart's dance, satyr girdled about with vines dancing on the holy obscenity of Silenus? Naked skeletal imprints, against the raw rock wall of a cave one hot afternoon phantoms of the stone . . .

. . . .

I listen. The fountains have gone silent under the voice of the wind. From the rocks a little string of water runs down to a hollowed-out place. The wind slacks off and softens the bite of distant sorrow. Here I am turned. From among the twilit rocks a black horned immobile shape watches me I too immobile with its golden eyes.

. . . .

Down there in the twilight the plain of Romagna. O woman I've dreamed over, woman adored, strong-minded woman, your profile ennobled by a memory of Byzantine stillness,

noble and mythic head in strong smooth lines
gilded by the enigma of sphinxes: twilit eyes in a
landscape of towers dreamed there on the banks
of the war-torn plain, on the banks of rivers
drunk down by the savage earth there where
Francesca's cry is lost forever: from my child-
hood a liturgical voice over and over intoned in
prayer slowly and movingly: and you from that
rhythm sacred to me and much moved arose, al-
ready restless with vast plains, with distant mi-
raculous destinies: my hope reawakens on the
endlessness of the plain or the sea when I feel a
breath of grace flutter: nobility incarnate and
golden, golden depth of your eyes: huntress,
lover, mystic, benign in human nobility ancient
Romagna.

. . . .

Water from the mill flows slowly and invisibly
into the millstream. I see a boy again, the same
boy, stretched out down there on the grass. He
appears to be sleeping. I think back on my own
childhood: how long it's been since magnetic
rays from the stars spoke to me for the first time
about the endlessness of the dead! . . . Time
has passed, growing thicker and larger, and
gone: just so the water goes by, not moving at all

for the boy down there: leaving behind it a silence, the millrace deep and unchanged: conserving the silence just as every day the shadow . . .

That boy or merely some likeness projected by my own nostalgia? So still down there: just like my own corpse.

Marradi (Ancient vault. Covered mirror)

Morning shines on the tops of all the mountains. High on the pinnacles of a desolate triangle the castle catches the light, higher and farther away. Venus goes by, crouched down in a two-wheeled cart on the street next to the convent. The river unknots in the valley: broken and lowing softly from time to time it sings and rests in huge blue mirrors: it runs more quickly along the black walls of rock (a red cupola, far off, laughs out with its lion), and the belltowers crowd together and in the blackening restlessness of the rooftops in sunlight a long veranda which has scribbled a many-colored comment with its arches!

Near Marradi (October)

I've fallen in with good people. The window of
my room gives out on the winds: and the . . .
and the son, poor little bird with sweet features
and indecisive spirit, poor little bird who drags a
broken leg, and the wind that beats at the win-
dow from the cloud-crowded horizon, the
mountains high and far away, the monotonous
rumble of the wind. In the distance snow has
fallen . . . the silent landlady makes up my
bed again helped by her young servant girl. Mo-
notonous sweetness of the patriarchial life. End
of the pilgrimage.

IMAGES FROM THE JOURNEY AND THE MOUNTAIN

After the stronger, second soul had broken our
    chains
In the deaf, night-long struggle,
We woke up crying and it was blue morning:
They sailed like the shadows of heroes:
Out of the dawn no shades fell in the pure
    silences
Out of the dawn
In the pure thoughts
No shades fell
Out of the dawn no shades:
Crying: swearing our faith to that blue

. . . .
. . . .

The woman sitting above the last steep
    ascent
Near the old house seems like a pale young girl
    still:

At her feet the valleys unknot uncertainly
Toward the high solitudes of the horizons:
So kind so old she hears the cuckoo singing.
And her simple heart tested over the years
By the melodies of the earth
Listens quietly: the notes
Come on, ambiguous and unbroken like veins in
a silk veil.
The swollen stream had risen out of the dark
woods
And in sluggish eddies and suck-pools skims the
rock edges,
Wrapping around the light blue of the air . . .
And the cuckoo lets fall, more slowly still, two
veiled notes
Into the pale blue silence

. . . .
. . . .

The air laughs: the valley trumpet
Blasts at the mountains: the outriders
Break loose: they move in quick leaps and
bounds: our hearts
Leap also: they shout and cross over the bridges.
And from the heights to the infinite dawns,
Vigilant, they come down anxiously through the
mountains,
Trembling and beautiful in the living fountains,

The echoes of our two submissive hearts . . .
They have crossed over in a long procession:
I don't know what drinking song they raise
In the air: and behind them the mountain thun-
    ders down:

. . . .
And one makes out their green song.

. . . .
To go, *from the waters to the whirlpools* down
The valley's slope, *in the muffled whisper caressing*
    me:
To follow down the valley's descent
A tired wing that beats and turns: to go
Desolate through valleys until, in a serenity
Of pale blue, rising out of the harsh rocks
A grey various village looms over me
Appearing and disappearing in alternating
    thoughts,
Above the barren dream, the sky cleared off!
O if like the stream that collapses
And rests in the smooth blue of itself,
If so at your walls the spirit declines
To nothing in its fatal going away,
If at your walls I could stretch out
In a crystalline peace, in a similar peace,
And mirror the memory of a divine
Lost serenity O you immortal

74

Spirit! O You!

. . . .
. . . .
Intent on the mysterious chorus of the wind
In roads of long tranquil waves,
Mute and glorious the harvest unbuttons the
    blouse
Of her golden lights in front of my very eyes.
O Hope! O Hope! By the tens of thousands
The summer fruits glisten and shine! a chorus
Enchanted, melodious in its own murmur,
Which lives by a myriad of sparks . . . !

Here is the night: and here to watch me
And lights and lights: and I far away and alone:
The harvest is quiet, toward infinity
(The spirit is quiet) poems go silently
Into the night: into the night: I mean: only
Shadow that comes back, that once was
    divided . . .

VOYAGE TO MONTEVIDEO

     I saw from the deck of the ship
The hills of Spain
Disappear, the brown earth
Hiding like melody in the green
Inside the golden twilight:
Out of an unknown scene, a girl alone
Like a blue
Song, a violet still trembling on the low
    hillside . . .
The evening drained off sea-color becoming
    sky-color:
Also the gilded silences from time to time of
    wings
Passed over slowly through the diaphanous
    blue . . .

From even more distant silences,
Golden far-away birds tinted in different colors
Crossed and recrossed in the powder blue eve-
    ning: the ship
Already blind plowing ahead beating against the
    darkness
With our shipwrecked hearts
Beating against the darkness its blue wings on
    the sea.
But one day
The serious matrons of Spain came on board
With their troubled angelic eyes
With their breasts heavy with vertigo. When
In the deep bay of an equatorial island
In a bay tranquil and deep much deeper than the
    night sky
We saw rising in the enchanted light
A white city asleep
Beneath the towering peaks of extinct volcanoes
In the vertiginous breath of the equator: until
After much shouting and many shadows from an
    unknown country,
After much clattering of chains and much fever-
    ish activity
We left the equatorial city
For the restless night-gathering sea.
We went on and on, for days and days: the ships

Heavy with slack sails in the hot wind-gusts passed
     slowly opposite us
Near us on the quarter-deck there appeared a sun-bronzed
Girl of the new race,
Her eyes luminous her clothes wind-whipped: and look:
     wild at the end of a day appears
The wild sea-coast down there above the endless
     ocean:
And I saw the dunes
Like dizzying mares that melted away
Into the endlessness of the grasslands
Deserted without a single human house
And we turned away fleeing the dunes where
     there appeared
On a yellow sea created by the prodigious abun-
     dance of the river,
The marine capital of the new continent.
The evening light was transparent new and
     electric
And the tall houses seemed empty there
Down there on the pirate's sea
Of the city abandoned
Between the yellow sea and the yellow dunes...
. . . .

FLORENCE

Florence, powerful lily, spring shoot. Spring
mornings along the Arno. The grace of adoles-
cents (that isn't grace to a world your own
Aprilic graces conquer), alive virgin continuous
breath, so fresh that it brings the marbles to life
and gives birth to the Botticellian Venus: the
pollens of desire heavy with all the carved forms
of beauty, the high spiritual Heaven, the out-
lines of wandering hills, together with the sharp
nostalgia of disappearance exhaled by beauty's
whiter forms: also the divine feeling of being
beyond music is ours, in the peopled dream of
plastic images!

Here the Arno has fresh ripplings still: later it takes on the silence of deeper places: in the channels between low monotonous hills nudging the little Etruscan cities, level now all the way to its mouth, leaving behind the white trophies of Pisa, the precious duomo traversed with its colossal beams, holding in its nakedness such vast breath from the sea. At Signa in the continuous assonant musical humming I remember that deep silence: silence of a buried epoch, silence of a buried civilization: and as a young Etruscan girl is able to sadden the landscape . . .

In the narrow central street, taverns with bad reputations, secondhand shops, strange mismatched brasses. One tavern that's always deserted during the daytime flourishes at night, a great bustle of sinister figures behind the glass. Shouts and mockery and brutal insults spill out in the street whenever some adventurer goes in. Facing the short twisting street is a single window, one only, behind an iron grille in the corroded red wall of an old palazzo, where the stupid-looking ruined whores press up against the bars with their heavily rouged faces giving them the tragic look of clowns. That empty passageway, fetid from its urinal and the mold on its corroded walls, has the tavern finally as its only view. The overly-made-up clowns seem to follow the life that unfolds behind the glass windows with great curiosity, the smoke from the sour-smelling pasta, the laughter of the men kept by their women and the sudden silences caused by the arrival of the vice squad: Three under-age girls sway their precocious graces monotonously back and forth. Three hirsute Germans lank and down at the heels sit as though composed around a liter of wine. One of them with a Christlike face is dressed in priest's robes (!) which he keeps gathered up on his knees. Sour steam from the pasta: clatter of plates and plink of glasses: laughter of men whose fingers are covered with rings who let themselves be caressed by their women, now they have eaten. The serving girls pass by in the air sour from the smoke fumes giving out a musical shout: pasta, pasta. In a black and white picture a dark girl with a guitar shows her teeth and the whites of her eyes rolled back. — Serenade on the quays of the Arno. A tired breath of wind runs over me from the Florentine hills: it brings with it the smell of dulled crowns, mixed with an odor of lacquer and varnish from old paintings, just barely perceptible (Mereskowski).

FAENZA

A huge baroque tower: behind the balcony rail-
ing a lighted lamp: it looms up on the piazza at
the head of a long street in which all the palazzi
are red and all have corroded balconies: (the
quarters where the street curves are all de-
serted). Some matrons full of charm. In the air a
gathering sense of dancing. I listen: the huge ba-
roque tower now lit up gives a sense of freedom
a sense of liberation to the air. The transparent
eye of the clock overhead seems to light up the
evening, its hands gilded: a small white ma-
donna shows herself now behind the balcony
railing where the little corroded lantern is lit:
*And already the huge, baroque tower is empty and you
can see that it contains, illuminated, the symbols of time
and faith.*

The piazza has a stage-like quality with its loggias and white arches so delicate so strong. The poor fishwife passes the café-concert scenery, nets on her head and a fine black shawl over her thin shoulders fastened with black catches; she walks all the way through the piazza alive with its delicate strong arches. Nearby someone throws a black net shaped like a three-cornered hat over one shoulder which comes uncovered: a dark, aquiline, questioning face, similar to Michelangiolo's figure of Night.

. . . .

Ophelia my landlady is pale and her long eyelashes just fringe her eyes: her face is both classic and adventurous. I notice she bites her lips: like the Spanish, like the Italian sweetness: and at the same time: the memory, the reflection: *like the youth of ancient Rome*. I listen to the talk. Life here has a strong naturalistic sense. As it does in Spain. The happiness of living in a town without philosophy.

The museum. Ribera and Baccarini. In the main body of the old red palazzo fire-hot in the noontide the shadow smoulders on the rough wall where skeletal nude engravings hang. Dürer,

Ribera. Ribera: the satyr's dance-step sharp on the obscene drunken Silenus. The echo of dried-out melodies clearly ebbing back in the deaf shadow. Young girls in sailor suits, their smooth legs milk-white going by now and then dragging along and thrust on by a vague white itch. The delicate bust of a young man, smiling joyous light of the Italian spirit, a white virginal purity preserved in the delicate carving of the marble. Great figures of the classic tradition keep their strength closed between their eyelids.

SCIROCCO

(Bologna)

Was it a melody, was it a gust of breath? Something was out there on the other side of the glass. I opened the window: Scirocco: and some clouds hurrying across the curved bottom of the sky (wasn't the sea down there?) heaped up in a silverish splendor where sunrise had left a gilded memento. All around the city was showing off colossal cross-beams and roof timbers in the open scaffolding of its large towers, still damp from the recent rain that had darkened its brick and tile: it gave off the image of a great port, deserted and clouded over, its granaries still open after the adventurous departure of the morning: while in the scirocco the golden reflections of the flags and ships that rode the curve of the horizon seemed down there to keep on arriving still in hot and distant breaths. You felt the anticipation. In the hubbub of tranquil voices the silvery tones of the children rose easily above all the rest in the drying air. The city was resting after its feverish work. It was the eve of a holiday: Christmas Eve. I felt that everything was resting: memories hopes expectations I too abandoned them to the curved horizon down there: and the horizon seemed to me to want to rock them and lull them in the tasseled lightspokes reflecting in its clouds metamorphosing into infinity. I was free, I was alone. I reveled in the joyfulness of the scirocco and its tenuous breathing. I saw the wintery overcast that dissolved before it: the clouds that flected and reflected their silvery flashes off the splotched paving stones onto the wispy pearl-colored luminescence of female faces triumphant in their dark sweet eyes: under the opening of the porticoes I followed the beautiful women with their melodious plumes, I heard their melodious footsteps, muffled in a light and even cadence: later I looked at the red towers with their black beams, with their open balustrades which looked out deserted on infinity.

It was Christmas Eve.

*

I had gone out: a great red portico with Moorish lanterns: books I had read in my adolescence were displayed in a window among engravings. At the far end the marble splendor of a grand modern building, curved strips of steel enclosing white globes at each of its four corners.

The little piazza of S Giovanni was deserted: the prison doorway without the young working girls I'd seen on other occasions.

*

A young woman coming across a piazza gilded by little burial vaults in the white wake of her own hat plume, grey eyes, mouth with a thin red lip line, walked past me in the immense pearl-shine from the sky. The melodic line of her footsteps bleached out and disappeared in the smoky daylight. Something new, something childish and deep, was in the charged air. The red brick rejuvenated by the rain seemed to exhale troubled uneasy ghosts, caught up in a shadow of original sorrow, passing by in their own troubled dream: (contiguous and even the arches losing

87

themselves step by step in the landscape among the hills beyond the gate): then a great line that appeared passed by: the magnificent, virginal inclined head of a maidservant borne along by a sassy young step not tamed yet by any established cadence, offering up the profile of a strong rose-colored jawline and from time to time the shifting light-shafts of a dark eye over her menial shoulder and arm, the smoulderings of youth; silently.

*

(The simple housemaids busied with their shopping nets full of food wandered about primping in the fresh joy of their release outside the doors of the house. The countryside all around completely green. The great smoky masses of trees lowered their weights on the small hills, their outline against the sky adding a note of fantasy: a barrel-organ that tried out the modest poetry of the people under a huge smokestack on the lovely fields, the light among the varicolored women beside the doors: the dark quarters of the city alive and swarming with red tentacles: tower verandas with their enormous beams under the curved sky: the last reflected hot and distant breaths blowing across the great splendor dazzling and constant when I go forward under the gate's arc out into the green and the cannon thundered noon: alone with the sparrows around me, who moved in short flutters and whirls about the Leonardine lake.)

PIAZZA SARZANO

Streets and streets go up to the old piazza where the tournaments were held and where you can look beyond to the sea in the pure air under heaven. The pure air is just marked out by the quick clouds. The air is rose-colored. An ancient twilight has brush-stroked the piazza and its walls. And lasts under the sky that lasts, rose-colored summer of an even more rose-colored summer.

In the twilit air you hear a serene laughter, and from the walls a small rose-colored tower hiding a bell juts out of the ivy: nearby, a fountain under a little cupola spurts out water water and more water effortlessly without hurry, at its top the blind bust of a wise Roman emperor: water, water, water spurts out effortlessly, and at its top the blind bust of a wise Roman emperor.

On the other side of the piazza a colored vertex takes on a pattern of little squares, from under its four spires a turret shows off assorted little glazed enamel squares, a sharp laugh in the sky, out past the cooing, above the little streets the red veil of the rose-red tile squares: and at that laugh I hear oblivion answers back. The same oblivion so dear to the statue of the pagan emperor at the top of the little cupola where the water gushes out in no hurry under the blind stare of the wise Roman emperor.

*

From the bridge above the city rhythmic Mediterranean cadences. The hills appear barren to me with their towers cutting through the green bars but down below the innumerable butterflies of the house lights fill up the landscape with an unmovable and inexhaustible joy. The large rose-colored houses among the meandering greenery continue to elude the twilight. On the cobblestones of the piazza a shrill rhythm is shouted out: a young boy who runs away melodiously in leaps and bounds. A glimmering at the far end of the vast desert of the piazza rises tortuously from the sea where the little streets green with mold fall away into the pit-traps of shadow: in the middle of the piazza, the eyeless head that looks out from the top of the cupola is cut off. A woman in white appears at an open window. Mediterranean night.

*

From the other side of the piazza the quadrangular tower rises in light from corroded brick at the top of the dark swollen tortuous alleyways palpitating in flame. The four-spired summit with the various little square enamel tiles laughs while in the white troubled background lechery sits imperiously next to the green lamp posts. Alongside the bust with the white and empty rose-colored eyes, and the clock high over the piazza green as a button that hooks up the correct time to the eternity of the piazza. The street twists and goes under. Like clouds on the hills the houses sail on still through the changing green and behind everything you just make out the trophy of the V.M. completely white and vibrating from its preened wings in the air.

GENOA

After the cloud came to a dead stop
Far-off in the sky above the silent infinite
Seacoast closed up in its own distant veils of
      mist,
And the departed soul came back
For everything around her was already arcane-
      ly lit up green dream of the garden
In the supernatural appearance
Of her shining superb statues:
And I heard singing I heard the voice of poets
In the fountains and the benign sphinxes on the
      pediments
Appeared to still lavish a first oblivion on those
Bowed down: I went out
From the secret labyrinths: a white towering
Loomed up in the air: innumerable from the sea
The white dreams of morning appeared
In the distance unshackling and shackling their
      chains
Like an unknown whirlwind of sound.
I heard the sound between the heaves of the
      spray-sails.
The May sun was ripe and full.

*

Under the oriental tower, on the green terraces
    on the ash-colored slate
The piazza spreads out like a lake toward the in-
    exhaustible ship-gathering sea
The arched red palazzo laughs from behind the
    enormous portico:
Like Niagara Falls
All its iron-colored fertile symphony sings and
    laughs as it changes urgently toward the sea
Genoa sing your song!

*

Inside a porcelain grotto
Sipping coffee
I watched the crowd through the glass window
    climbing up
Rapidly among the vendors who stood like
    statues, holding
Out seafood their raucous cries falling weakly
On their motionless scales:
Thus I remember you still and I see you again
Imperial up the steep tumultuous hill
Toward the opened gate
Against the blue of evening,

Fantastic with mythic trophies
Among the bare towers thrusting into the clear
    sky,
The fever of primitive life
Hooked tight to you everywhere:
And through the scurrilous alleyways under the
    street lamps
The starling song of the prostitutes
And from far below the sea wind unceasingly.

*

Down through the alleyways of the port down
    through the street lamps
The wind hunted from the tangle of ships
Preludes throughout the two-sided evening:
The sea-front palazzi had white
Arabesques in the languorous shadow
And I and the two-sided night set out:
And I raised my eyes up to the thousand
And thousand and thousand benevolent eyes
Of the chimeras in the heavens. . . . .
When,
Melodiously
Rising from up above, the wind pretended to be
    a white vision of grace
As though from the tireless vicissitudes

Of the clouds and stars inside the evening sky
Inside the port alleys rising up above, ...
Inside the port alleys that rising up above
     reddened
The red wings of the street lamps
Ornamenting the languorous shadow with ara-
     besques, ...
That in the port alleyway, rising up above
Rose up white and light and peevishly!
"*As in the red wings of the street lamps*
Red and white in the shadow of the street lamp
It rose up white and light and quivering: . . ."
Already now in the red of the street lamp
The shadow was already laboriously
Whitening . . . .
Whitening while in the red of the street lamp
White distant laboriously
The amazed echo laughed an unreal
Laugh: and while the echo laboriously
And white and light and amazed rose up . . .
Already everywhere all
The two-sided evening glittered and flashed:
The street lamps pulsed
Like heartbeats in the shadow.
Far-off noises crumbled and slid
Into solemn silences
Asking: if laughter

Wasn't rising out of the sea . . .
Asking if evening
Indefatigably
Was listening to it: to the vicissitudes
Of the clouds up there
In the star-studded sky.

*

The little boat perches at the port's edge
In a twilight glittering
Among the calm trees dangling their fruits of
        light,
In the mythic landscape
Of ships on the breast of the infinite
In the evening
Balmy with happiness, luminously bristling
In a great in a great curtain
Of diamonds spread out on the twilight,
Thousands and thousands of diamonds in a great
        vibrant curtain
The little boat unloads
Uninterruptedly creaking
Untiringly deafening
And the flag is lowered and the sky and the sea
        are golden and on the jetty
The children run around and scream

With their shrill cries of happiness.
Now like shoals of fish travellers spread out
Into the thundering city
Which lays open its streets and piazzas:
The great Mediterranean light
Is melted and poured into the ash-colored stone:
Through ancient and deepening alleyways,
The roar of life, an intense and fugitive joy:
The sky is a golden curtain of happiness
Where the fabulous sun
Left his unpriceable booty

And the city understands
And lights up
And the flame titillates and absorbs
The magnificent residues of the sun,
And weaves a winding sheet
Of holy oblivion for tired men.
Lost in the thundering twilight
The shadows of travellers
Wander through La Superba
As terrible and grotesque as the blind.

*

Vast, in a thin and evaporating smell
Of tar, watched over by electric

Moons on a sea just barely alive
The vast port sleeps.
Smoke clouds rise from the chimneys
While the port sleeps in the sweet continuous
    creaking
Of ropes and lines: and now that its strength
Sleeps, what rocks and lulls its sadness sleeps also
Oblivious to what will come
As the vast port swings back and forth inside
An exhausted rhythm and one feels
The cloud starting to form out of its silent
    vomiting.

*

O arrogant opulent fallen Sicilian woman
In the wind-blown window of the portside street
In the heart of the city beaten by ship-sounds
    and wagon-sounds
Classic Mediterranean woman of the ports:
Through the grey-rose of the slate city
The noises of evening were ricocheting
And then they hushed into night-noises inside the
    serene dark:
I saw in front of the windows bright as stars
The shadows of dockside families pass back and
    forth and heard

The slow uncertain songs in the veins of the Med-
        iterranean city:
For the night was thick and deep.
While you Sicilian, from the hollow
Windows were enclosed
Up to your nipples in shadow
In a grim game
Of hollow shadow and flickering light
O Sicilian,
Octopus of the Mediterranean nights.
One of the port cranes creaked creaked creaked
        in its chains
In the hollow of the calm night
And in its iron arms
The weak heart beat with a louder throb: you
Had turned out the window light:
Naked mystical hollow above us
Infinitely sharp-eyed devastation: Tyrrhenian
        night.

TOSCANITÀ

For Bino Binazzi

"In order that this reality exist you must stretch a yellow vault over the black velvet and the braids of a weaver weaving dust-motes of gold.

Don't start up the embers of passion: they will answer you with the elemental fire of playing cards. But if instead you hear the drum beats the poor young Giotto accompanied his Madonnas with you'd better be sure those double planes will give you the solution to the double meaning that the spirit and pride anticipate."

GENOA WOMAN

You brought me a little seaweed
In your hair, and a wind odor
That came in from hundreds of miles away and
    arrives
Heavy with meaning, smuggled in your tanned
    skin:
— O the divine
Simplicity of your acrobat's body —
Not love not spasm, but something untouchable,
Necessity's ghost that walks aimlessly
Serene and ineluctable through the soul
And unties it with joy, as though under a sweet
    spell,
So that the desert wind
Can carry it out through infinity.
How small the world is
                and how light it is in your hands.

FURIOUS

I had embraced her.
While breathless in that blind elation
I groped blindly along its edges
Repeating the ever-quickening blows
Over the doorway of eternal grace:
Suddenly she rose up
And fell on me hammering her foot
Deafeningly and rhythmically across my back. It
    was the memory
Of a vanishing instant, the roll-call of death
Isolate in the amazing fulfillment.
Desperately gathering up my courage
I redoubled my efforts to that call
Prophetic and panting and crossed over into
The resting place of nothingness and elation,
    fiercely
Proudly, breaking her forehead open
Feverishly grabbing the woman's throat
Victorious then in the mystic manner
In my ancient country in the great Nothing.

IN THE MOUNTAINS

From the Falterona to Corniolo (deserted valleys)

To go and keep on going: the divine spirit
Grows dim: the mists of Fate
Press down: not ever then for the inclined
Forehead the wing of your flowered kiss
O beauty o you alone: to go and keep on going!
And the village appeared half-way up the
     mountain:
Above the rocks it towered white
And grey and in the other part of myself
     alternately toward him
The currents of life flowed . . .

O if like the stream that collapses at last
And rests in the smooth blue of itself,
If so at your walls the spirit declines
To nothing in its fatal going away,
If at your walls I could stretch out
In a crystalline peace, in a similar peace
And mirror the memory of a divine
Lost serenity, o my immortal
Spirit! . . .
But come to my senses I turned toward the sea:
Your peace struck me like a snake:
I cried out: may all my garlands be folded up
In the sadness of infinite bitter deaths . . .

ON THE POETRY OF CAMPANA
by Eugenio Montale

[Published in *L'Italia che scrive* (XXV, 9-10), Rome, September–October 1942. Montale's essay was written following the publication of a new, further enlarged edition of the *Canti orfici* and of a volume of Campana's *Inediti* (Unpublished Writings), both of them edited by Enrico Falqui.]

The publication of 2 whole volumes of uncollected writings by Dino Campana and the republication of the *Canti orfici* in a more accurate edition than the previous (1928) one offers a good pretext in several respects for re-examining the work of a poet who has not been forgotten. Campana's bibliography, which has already been carefully compiled by Falqui, will doubtless be added to by numerous writers. Yet, in contributing in our own small way to such an "increase," we soon find that there is not a great deal of uncovered territory. The poet of Marradi was not unappreciated; and if, in his opinion, help and assistance of a more concrete nature did not accompany this appreciation before he was struck by an incurable "spiritual confusion," he was not alone in suffering such a fate. Much is permitted to dead poets, little to the living: especially to the living with the troublesome nature of Campana. Proud, sick, and restless as he was, who could have calmed him and brought him peace? Strictly speaking, I repeat, there was no lack of appreciation. When, between November 1915 and May 1916, Campana published in *Riviera Ligure* the five poems which Binazzi added to the 1928 edition of the *Canti orfici,* and which the present dedicated editor, Enrico Falqui, has placed among the uncollected poems (with the necessary note, it is true, though for our part we would have preferred a more strict distinction between those poems published by the author and the rest), the curiosity that had been aroused by the *Canti orfici* showed no signs of abating. The book had been praised by De Robertis, Binazzi, Boine, and Cecchi. Campana was thirty then, and in those days reviews were not measured in meters. In 1917 I myself came to know a group of student officers who were confirmed "Campanians" in the barracks of the Palazzo della Pilotta in Parma; the acknowledged leader of the group was Francesco Meriano, already editor of *La Brigata* and a friend of Binazzi. But in 1918 Campana was placed permanently in a sanatorium, and it was then that his myth was born. Since then, articles on the *Canti orfici* have followed one after another, among the most notable of which for me are those by Solmi, Gargiulo, Contini, and Bo, all of them listed, along with many others, in Falqui's bibliography. In these writings one can see plainly the double interpretation of Campana which was already latent in his earliest critics, and which finally attained perfect clarity of expression in Contini's essay. Is Campana a *visual* or a *visionary* poet? A recent rereading of the *Canti orfici* has convinced me — let me say right away — that the horns of this dilemma are anything but irreconcilable: for it's true that Campana's critics who are least inclined to mysticism and irrationalism concede him "illuminations pushed to the point of myth" (Gargiulo) and deny that in Campana it is possible to speak of simple impressionism (Contini); while on the other hand the most astute interpreter of the poet's "uncontrollable night" (Carlo Bo) has expressed himself in phrases and images ("a poetry that did not have the time to flower, or did so only with the too-early, cruel assistance of its fruits") which reveal at least one limit of this poetry.

The observation, which is easy enough to make even if it were not confirmed by personal recollection, that Campana was soon noticed by the establishment, must not lead one to think that the rumor-mongers of the moment (futurists, Lacerbians,[1] etc.) paid much attention to the author of the *Canti orfici*. They may have taken him for one of their own, but at a proper distance; and Campana himself did not regard them with great sympathy. Still, the poet did not sprout like a mushroom in an atmosphere unprepared to receive him. One of the interesting aspects of the uncollected work just published (about sixty poems, along with various notes, aphorisms, pensées, etc.) is precisely that it allows us to relate Campana better to his times and shed light on his futurist apprenticeship. An apprenticeship about which there had always been explicit and implicit doubts. Today the weakest parts of the *Inediti* [*Unpublished Writings*], and especially of the forty-four poems in

---

1. *Lacerba* was a futurist-oriented literary and political review founded by Giovanni Papini and Ardengo Soffici upon their leaving *La Voce* in 1913. The magazine suspended publication in 1915.

the recently discovered notebook, convince us that the poet began and developed anything but precociously, in an atmosphere red-hot with isms. The list of poems that contain striking traces of the work in Marinetti's first anthology of 1912 would not be short. They range from a "tentacular" Marinetti-Buzzi[2] ambience (*"O poesia poesia," "Oh l'anima vivente," "Umanità fervente sulla sprone,"* etc.) to an Art Nouveau-style symbolism, somewhere between Lucini[3] and D'Annunzio (*"Convito romano egizio"* and others). There are also signs of the "loutish" Palazzeschi[4] (*"Prosa fetida"*) sometimes allied with the scene-painting of Rosai[5] (*"Notturno teppista"*). (We shall mention a different Palazzeschi later on.) But the group also contains poems which will be significant when set next to those

---

2. Paolo Buzzi (b. 1874). Futurist poet and novelist.

3. Gian Pietro Lucini (1867-1914). Poet, novelist, and essayist. A futurist with a sensual, D'Annunzian love of language, he was the author of *Il verso libero* [*Free Verse*] (1908).

4. Aldo Palazzeschi. Pseudonym of Aldo Giurlani (1884-1974). Originally a crepuscular poet, he was briefly a futurist, working on *Lacerba* with Papini and Soffici, and later wrote novels with surrealist overtones.

5. Ottone Rosai (1895-1957). Painter and writer. Originally a futurist, he later painted contemplative realist pictures in the nineteenth-century Tuscan tradition.

of the *Orfici:* "*Donna genovese,*" "*Il ritorno,*" "*Sulle montagne,*" for example. There is also the typical Campanian musical *Stimmung* a little bit everywhere ("*A un angelo del Costa,*" "*Furibondo,*" "*Une femme qui passe*" . . .) which we shall see later in *La chimera.* As well as that vast Mediterranean sense of space which is typical of certain of Campana's efforts, here, naturally, not without a great deal of D'Annunzio.

Are these juvenile poems? Up to a point. In all probability, the poems in the notebook were written between 1912 and 1914 when the poet was between twenty-seven and twenty-nine. Perhaps they were all transcribed quickly and at once, making use of recent experiences (recollections of his trip to South America in March-November 1913) as well as others less recent, so that they wouldn't be lost. It's impossible to know for certain. The most achieved poems of the *Orfici,* the only ones that stay in one's memory, are almost all here; or their musical germ is here. Campana appears to have included them in the *Orfici* without looking at the notebook again. And when we remember that after the manuscript of the *Orfici* was lost Campana rewrote it very speedily, it is possible to conclude that the rewriting-transcribing of the parts of the notebook included in the *Orfici* must also have been rapid: rapid, and followed, if not by a repudiation, then certainly by dissatisfaction and disinterest. Clearly the notebook was put away for what Campana thought would be forever.[6] We know nothing of the manuscript of the *Orfici* that was lost; nor how far the recopied manuscript followed the old one in terms of the prose pieces it contained. But we can conclude that here too Campana had worked *ex novo* and quickly, since it is true that they represent the maturest part, even in a stylistic sense, of the book. Campana saved only a small part of the earlier poems represented wholly or in part by the notebook — clearly the best part, thus proving himself a perceptive critic of himself. In any case it is clear that — whether from memory or not — Campana clipped the verse part of the *Orfici* out of his notebook, and in clipping the poems, he pruned and lightened them. His idea of a "European, musical, colorful" poetry was a product of Campana's education as well as an instinct; but it clearly had been accompanied or preceded by an experimentation, still somewhat inert and passive with the new isms then in the

---

6. It was found later. [Author's note.]

air. Official Futurism, too, like the earlier inno-
vators at the turn of the century, had claimed
that it was "breaking the glass," clearing the
air. Campana, however, had chosen subtler
masters than those followed by his temporary
mentors. He instinctively rejected the more me-
chanical, cataloguing aspect of the free verse
that was then fashionable, and went — as the
facts confirm — to the truest sources of the
movement from Whitman to Rimbaud. He him-
self related an issue of style to an issue of con-
science, in art as in life, and he was aware that in
his time and place his was a new and different
voice. But we should be careful not to attribute
too much conscious reflection to a man who,
due to the tragic and precarious state of his
health, was the poet of a brief, perhaps ex-
tremely brief, period. One of the charms of
Campana's poetry certainly lies in its obscurity,
which was anything but intentional, but which
the poet's illness protected and favored. It is a
poetry — here I share the opinion of Solmi —
"which can hardly be separated from the fever-
ish atmosphere which is its source." Gargiulo
seems to feel otherwise: he points out the poet's
obscurities and declares that "nothing, on the
page, authorizes us to make biographical deduc-

114

tions as to the causes of this defect: on the page we can attribute it only, as in similar cases, to the profundity or 'ineffability' of its inspiration." It is not entirely clear what similar cases Gargiulo has in mind. The reference to ineffability would make one think of Ungaretti; but it is clear that in Ungaretti the danger of obscurity is accepted, even theoretically, as the inevitable counterpart of a risky desire for pure poetry which is much less apparent in Campana. Ungaretti, who has qualities all his own which distinguish him from his epigones and imitators, clearly shares the taste for the fragment understood as a new genre, perhaps the only genre of our time, a legitimate and self-sufficient expression of the lyric *moment*, the product of a poetics which does not wish to mix the necessarily brief and flashing apparitions of poetry with elements of a different, voluntary nature. Up to a point, Campana belongs to this climate: among his obscure intentions one can make out a demiurge, the ritualism of a conjurer of poetry who probably never would have been satisfied in the level of pure lyric. His is a poetry in flight, which always disintegrates at the point of completion: its development would have been unpredictable, to say the least. For the idea of what would have followed, that is, the idea of a later, *different* Campana is somehow unthinkable to us, and even unlikely. And in fact no one has dared to confront it, very few have considered Campana as a promising poet, cut short by an evil fate.

It has been observed that Campana was in better form in prose than in poetry. This is an accurate observation, but it cannot be forced. Campana the poet per se lacked time, application, and continuity, i.e., the very conditions which allow a poet, when he is not an *enfant prodigue* (as he was not), to perfect his instrument. Still, Campana's verse, even that part which is most open to classicizing movements, often justifies itself as a type or a variety of his prose. If it is important in a poet to cultivate the point of contact or coincidence between instinct (physiology) and technique, a close examination would permit us to observe the scant difference, which is not always a difference in tone, that lies between the two modes. Still, it remains true that — whether or not he cultivated them — Campana achieved the conditions of spontaneity in which he was able to express himself more often and more easily in his prose writings: writings

116

which run from the lowest, most diaristic tone, to the most elevated, which is not always his most poetic. It also seems probable, if not certain, that Campana was very unsure of his verse, since when he wrote or rewrote the prose sections of the *Orfici*, though he did not omit the poems in the notebook, he made a strict selection from them and revised them with great insight. As to the selection itself, we have already seen that, apart from the few exceptions indicated, it was made with rare clearsightedness; concerning the revisions, it is enough to examine the most conspicuous example, "*Boboli*," which appears this way in the notebook:

Nel giardino spettrale
Dove il lauro reciso
Spande spoglie ghirlande sul passato,
Nella sera autunnale,
Io lento vinto e solo
Ho il tuo profumo biondo rievocato.
Dalle aride pendici
Aspre, arrossate ne l'ultimo sole
Giungevano i rumori
Rauchi già di una lontana vita.
Io sulle spoglie aiuole

Io t'invocavo: o quali le tue voci
Ultime furon, quale il tuo profumo
Più caro, quale il sogno inquieto
Quale it vertiginoso appassionato
Ribelle sguardo d'oro?
S'udiva una fanfara
Straziante salire; il fiume in piena
Portava silenzioso
I riflessi dei fasti d'altri tempi.
Io mi affaccio a un balcone
E mi investe suadente
Tenero e grandioso
Fondo e amaro il profumo dell'alloro:
Ed ella m'è presente
(Tra le statue spettrali nel tramonto).[7]

---

7. In the spectral garden / where the cut laurel / spreads barren garlands on the past, / in the autumn evening / I, slow, defeated, alone, / called up your blond scent again. / From the rough, dry / slopes, red in the last of the sun, / came the now-harsh / noise of a far-off life. / I, in the barren flowerbeds / I invoked you: o what were / your last words, what your favorite / scent, your most disturbed dream / your giddy, passionate / rebellious golden look? / A heartbreaking fanfare / was heard rising: the flooding river / silently carried / the reflection of the splendor of other times. / I come out on a balcony / and persuasive, tender / majestic, deep and bitter / the scent of laurel fills me: / and she is here with me / (among the spectral statues in the sunset).

In the *Canti orfici*, it becomes the following, with the title "*Giardino autunnale*":

Al giardino spettrale al lauro muto
De le verdi ghirlande
A la terra autunnale
Un ultimo saluto!
A l'aride pendici
Aspre arrossate nell'estremo sole
Confusa di rumori
Rauchi grida la lontana vita:
Grida al morente sole
Che insanguigna le aiuole.
S'intende una fanfara
Che straziante sale: il fiume spare
Ne le arene dorate: nel silenzio
Stanno le bianche statue a capo i ponti
Volte: e le cose già non sono più.
E dal fondo silenzioso come un coro
Tenero e grandioso
Sorge ed anela in alto al mio balcone:
E in aroma d'alloro,
In aroma d'alloro acre languente,
Tra le statue immortali nel tramonto
Ella m'appar, presente.[8]

---

8. To the spectral gardens, to the silent laurel / with its green garlands, / to the autumn land / a last farewell! / On the dry

This is the most detached and perfect of Campana's lyrics: but such crystallization is rare for him. More often the poet seems tempted by *Lied*, even if it is a stuttering *Lied*, verging on the inexpressible:

Sorgenti sorgenti abbiam da ascoltare,
Sorgenti, sorgenti che sanno
Sorgenti che sanno che spiriti stanno
Che spiriti stanno ad ascoltare . . .[9]

Elsewhere much greater ambitions, compositional as well as musical, prevail: *"La chimera," "Immagini del viaggio e della montagna," "Viaggio a Montevideo," "Genova"*— thematically valuable, but only in places. Nevertheless, these poems show the direction which Campana the poet

---

slopes / Rough, red in the last sun / far-off life / blending in harsh noise / shouts to the dying sun / that bloodies the flower-beds. / A heartbreaking fanfare / is heard to rise: the river disappears / in the golden sands: in the silence / the white statues atop the bridges / have turned: and things no longer exist. / And from below, silence like a horn / Tender and majestic / rises and reaches toward my balcony: / and in the aroma of laurel, / the bitter, fading aroma of laurel, / among the immortal statues in the sunset / she appears to me, is here.

9. Springs springs we have to listen, / Springs, springs that know / Springs that know what spirits / what spirits are here to listen . . .

was consciously planning to take: the path from his most Lacerbian poems (*"Batte botte"*), passing close to the rhythmical experiments of Palazzeschi — with that breath rising to a double alexandrine time which Renato Serra[10] found in the poet of *"Gioco proibito"* — and hoping to arrive at a complete coloristic-musical dissolution of poetic discourse. Campana's interest in a poem of Giaconi's[11] (her *"Dianora,"* which was later attributed to him), and the letter he sent to Novaro[12] (in which he refers to "the neo-Greek sensibility of truly modern Italian poetry"), tell us something about this: Giaconi had been weaned on the English, and in her case the remark was certainly valid. On the path Campana had set out on, prose may have distracted and attracted him through the greater sense of freedom and agility it offered his volubility of expression — prose, certainly, as well as other occasional momentary distractions. In a lyric written after the *Orfici*, one of his last in verse,

10. (1884-1915). Literary critic, contributor to *La Voce*. Author of *Le lettere,* 1914. He was killed in World War I.

11. Luisa Giaconi (1870-1908). Poet, influenced by Pascoli. Her *Tebaide* was posthumously published in 1909.

12. Mario Novaro (1868-1944). Poet, editor of *Riviera Ligure* 1895-1919. He also edited the works of Boine.

"Hai domati i picchi irsuti," there are even some
choral and popular notes not far from parts of
Jahier.[13]

An urgency of content flashed into the uncon-
trollable night; the energetic will and volup-
tuousness of a nomad, a "tramp" who knew
Whitman and Rimbaud and experimented with
his poetry as an activity that was indivisibly
both aesthetic and voluntary, moral; "song of
himself"; *"saison en enfer"*; Lacerbian and Vo-
cean free verse and autobiography; diffuse neo-
classical echoes — De Robertis has mentioned
Carducci, and the idea of a traditional poet de-
stroyed by sickness or bad training has also been
suggested here and there — echoes not only of
Carducci but of D'Annunzio, which for my part
I would not want to separate from the more per-
sonal and obscure nature of Campana's "bar-
barous" message, from that idea of an Orphic
poetry which is not confined to the title of his
book and cannot be considered irrelevant to his
conception of himself as a latter-day Germanic
rhapsode, seduced and dazzeld by the bright

---

13. Piero Jahier (1884-1966). Autobiographical Genoese writ-
er, a member of the *Voce* group.

lights of the Mediterranean — all of this appears in flashes in the few pages of the *Canti orfici.*

Let us pause for a moment at this "Orphism," which Campana's book certainly makes no effort to define. It coincides with the rise of a metaphysical painting in Italy (Carrà, De Chirico) of whose existence and intentions Campana could not have been unaware. Like the early De Chirico, he evokes powerfully the ancient cities of Italy: Bologna, Faenza, Florence, and Genoa shine forth in his poems and inspire some of his greatest moments. Is this barbarous or if you will antique aspect another indication perhaps of his latent Carduccianism, which is even more apparent in the openings of some couplets? Possibly; but it seems to me that Campana's Orphism and his illusion that he was a latter-day *poeta germanicus* lost in the lands of the south clash in his intentions and even in his results. I have no wish to make Campana into a German poet except metaphorically, or into a theoretician of racism, but it was clearly not by chance that he dedicated the first edition of the *Orfici* to the "tragedy of the last German in Italy," and that in his dream of barbarism — which may have been nothing more than his incorrigible conviction that he was an ancient — there was actually a suggestion of an ideological and moral order. The disparate pensées (*Storie*) published in the recent *Inediti* includes several curious allusions to this: "The creator of French impressionism is the *gaulois*, a scoundrel who has become self-aware through democracy, a slave, incapable of abstract, i.e., aristocratic, ideas. The human odor of the *gaulois* is what makes France uninhabitable for delicate sensibilities. — Nietzsche." Other remarks follow which are also useful in interpreting his poetry: "To flow over life, this would be necessary,[14] this is the only possible art," and there are other references to Nietzsche and Wagner. But there is little, too little for one to make out anything like Campana's "thought." We do not know precisely how much German the poet knew: certainly it must have been among the five languages which he claimed to know well when he wrote to Novaro. He probably knew little or nothing of George, and the Orphic Rilke postdates his book; perhaps he had some awareness of Hölderlin's Greece; with Nietzsche he had a secure and often obsessive familiarity. In any case it is obvious that his

---

14. Here Campana is translating from the *Gay Science* of Nietzsche. [Author's note.]

sense of escape, "that investigation of dimen-
sion, that spatial tension" (Contini) was not
achieved — at times, it is true — without the
help of a language which vies with German in its
abstract capacities, an unfocused language, blunt
at the edges, capable of halos and iridescences,
of an "extremely bloated and never definite"
speech (Bo); the one language which could
render the *Stimmung* of *"La chimera," "Notte,"*
and many other fragments — at times, even, in
the notebook, in fragments of fragments, of a
more or less Futurist intonation. Is Campana a
poeta germanicus, then? And why not, if we re-
main in the realm of metaphor and admit that
Campana instinctively excavated for himself,
out of our language, a language entirely his
own? I have said "excavated" but actually it is
not the notion of an excavation that best de-
scribes Campana. We should think instead of ac-
tual leaps in the air, of rapid immersions in a
different element unfamiliar to the poet.

> *Dal ponte sopra la città odo le ritmiche cadenze*
> *mediterranee. I colli mi appaiono spogli colle loro*
> *torri a traverso le sbarre verdi ma laggiù le farfalle*
> *innumerevoli della luce riempono il paesaggio di*
> *una immobilità di gioia inesauribile. Le grandi case*

125

rosee tra i meandri verdi continuano a illudere il
crepuscolo. Sulla piazza acciottolata rimbalza un
ritmico strido: un fanciullo a sbalzi che sfugge mel-
odiosamente. Un chiarore in fondo al deserto della
piazza sale tortuoso dal mare dove vicoli verdi di
muffa calano in tranelli d'ombra: in mezzo alla
piazza, mozza la testa guarda senz'occhi sopra la
cupoletta. Una donna bianca appare a una finestra
aperta. È la notte mediterranea.[15]

There may be something of De Chirico here,
but dissolved in a Zarathustrian intoxication.
Note that this is not an extreme example, but
one of those which loses least in being taken out
of context. Let us see again, still choosing from
among the average examples, whether it is

---

15. From the bridge above the city I hear rhythmic Mediter-
ranean cadences. To me, the hills look barren with their towers
through the green bars but below the innumerable butterflies of
the lights fill the landscape with a stillness of inexhaustible joy.
The huge reddish houses among the green mazes continue to
elude the twilight. A rhythmic shout echoes on the cobbled pi-
azza: a child fleeing melodiously, by fits and starts. A brightness
beyond the desert of the piazza rises tortuous out of the sea
where green alleys of mold set in snares of shadow: in the midst
of the piazza, the eyeless severed head keeps watch from the
little cupola. A white woman comes to an open window. It's
Mediterranean night.

painting or music that dominates in apparently descriptive observations of this sort:

> *Tre ragazze e un ciuco per la strada mulattiera che scendono. I complimenti vivaci degli stradini che riparono la via. Il ciuco che si voltola in terra. Le risa. Le imprecazioni montanine. Le rocce e il fiume.*[16]

Is everything here? So it seems. But it is obvious that not even an extensive series of examples could make our metaphor visible, material. And yet we don't know what other key to offer to new readers of the *Orfici* than the recommendation that they take this poet's music in its native form, which is alive here and there throughout his work and especially in those mythic sketches — the return, the Mediterranean night, the image of Michelangelo, the backgrounds of that "divine primitive Leonardo" — when Campana pauses at the threshold of a door that doesn't open, or now and then opens only for him.

---

16. Three girls and a donkey, coming down the muletrack. Lively compliments from the roadmen lining the way. The donkey who rolls on the ground. Laughter. Mountain curses. The rocks and the river.

Beyond this, beyond these flights not only into space but also into the dimensions of a language which is born anew within another foreign, passive language entirely unaware of its latent capacity for transformation — and I am not referring to the language of Marinetti or the more human language of Soffici[17] — Campana's notebook would seem to have little lasting interest for us, and the objections of many of his critics would seem more than legitimate.

Campana has nothing to fear from a selection which would preserve his truest gift: his *diversity* of tone. It's true: the message of the *voyant* may leave us unconvinced, vague as it is; in his work "we are given to encounter neither the cultural drama nor the explosive religious anxiety of a Hölderlin" (Solmi); nor, let us add, the blaze of light of a Blake, nor the subterranean thematic unity of a Rimbaud. It is easy to admit that Campana was working toward structures and perspectives that were very different from those to be found in the *chimismi*[18] of his time; but it is

---

17. Ardengo Soffici (1879-1964). Futurist writer and painter. Founded the futurist review *Lacerba* with Papini in 1913. A Fascist, he was elected to the Italian Academy in 1939.

18. A *chimismo* is the complex of chemical processes which together make up a physiological function. *Chimismi lirici* was the title of a well-known book by Soffici published in 1915.

also clear that he was not a lyric poet in the exclusive sense, *tout entier à sa proie attaché*. The sense of limitation, of obstacle, is rare in him; he was fought over and visited by too many abstract possibilities; his own notion of a musical, colorful European poetry sounds a bit vague today. The poet has need of a decisiveness of an almost physical nature, the impossibility of expressing himself in any other way. And this decisiveness, which at a certain point coincides with an artist's greatest spontaneity, we find above all in Campana's prose. If it were not repugnant to reduce to shreds a spirit who aimed at total expression and yet has left us with such a fragmentary picture of himself, we might be inclined to abridge Campana's work, which is already so short, limiting it to a few incorruptible pages in which we feel it is impossible to deny that the poet of Marradi had a voice very different from those of his time. An anthology which would include, for example, *"La notte," "La Verna," "Firenze," "Scirocco," "Piazza Sarzano," "Faenza,"* a few of the nocturnes, some of the poems already mentioned, and a few other fragments and pensées. Is it little? Is it poetry in prose and therefore base in tone? Let's forget the "therefore," I don't believe it necessarily follows. Dino Campana, who, as Cecchi has said, "passed

129

like a comet," may not have exercised "an in-
calculable influence," but the traces of his pass-
ing are anything but buried in sand. There was
nothing mediocre in him; even his errors I
would not call errors but inevitable collisions
with the sharp corners that awaited him at every
step. The collisions of a blind man, if you will.
Visionaries, even if they happen to be "visual"
like our Campana, are inevitably the most art-
less, the blindest of creatures on this earth.

translated by Jonathan Galassi